# Greater Than a Tourist Book Series
## Reviews from Readers

I think the series is wonderful and beneficial for tourists to get information before visiting the city.

-Seckin Zumbul, Izmir Turkey

I am a world traveler who has read many trip guides but this one really made a difference for me. I would call it a heartfelt creation of a local guide expert instead of just a guide.

-Susy, Isla Holbox, Mexico

New to the area like me, this is a must have!

-Joe, Bloomington, USA

This is a good series that gets down to it when looking for things to do at your destination without having to read a novel for just a few ideas.

-Rachel, Monterey, USA

Good information to have to plan my trip to this destination.

-Pennie Farrell, Mexico

Great ideas for a port day.

-Mary Martin USA

Aptly titled, you won't just be a tourist after reading this book. You'll be greater than a tourist!

-Alan Warner, Grand Rapids, USA

Even though I only have three days to spend in San Miguel in an upcoming visit, I will use the author's suggestions to guide some of my time there. An easy read - with chapters named to guide me in directions I want to go.

-Robert Catapano, USA

Great insights from a local perspective! Useful information and a very good value!

-Sarah, USA

This series provides an in-depth experience through the eyes of a local. Reading these series will help you to travel the city in with confidence and it'll make your journey a unique one.

-Andrew Teoh, Ipoh, Malaysia

# GREATER THAN A TOURIST- MINNESOTA USA

*50 Travel Tips from a Local*

Marc H. Friedman

Cover designed by: Ivana Stamenkovic
Cover Image: https://pixabay.com/en/voyageurs-national-park-park-usa-347379/

CZYK Publishing Since 2011.

Greater Than a Tourist
Visit our website at www.GreaterThanaTourist.com

Lock Haven, PA
All rights reserved.
**ISBN:** 9781724129352

# &gt;TOURIST

## 50 TRAVEL TIPS FROM A LOCAL

# BOOK DESCRIPTION

Are you excited about planning your next trip?

Do you want to try something new?

Would you like some guidance from a local?

If you answered yes to any of these questions, then this Greater Than a Tourist book is for you.

Greater Than a Tourist- Minnesota, USA by Marc Friedman offers the inside scoop on the Twin Cities of Minneapolis and St. Paul, as well as outstate highlights around the rest of beautiful Minnesota. Most travel books tell you how to travel like a tourist. Although there is nothing wrong with that, as part of the Greater Than a Tourist series, this book will give you travel tips from someone who has lived at your next travel destination.

In these pages, you will discover advice that will help you throughout your stay. This book will not tell you exact addresses or store hours but instead will give you excitement and knowledge from a local that you may not find in other smaller print travel books.

Travel like a local. Slow down, stay in one place, and get to know the people and the culture. By the time you finish this book, you will be eager and prepared to travel to your next destination.

# TABLE OF CONTENTS

# DEDICATION

This book is dedicated to my father, Arnold S. Friedman, who instilled in me a love of writing at a very young age. As a newspaper editor in New York City and Massachusetts, he opened my eyes to the world around me, impressing upon me the importance of honesty and accuracy.

# ABOUT THE AUTHOR

Marc Friedman is a New York City native who moved to   Minnesota in 1983. He lives just minutes from downtown Minneapolis in the suburb of St. Louis Park.  While raised in an enormous city, Marc not only loves the hustle and bustle of city life, but the great outdoors, and Minnesota is the perfect place to experience them both. From the Twin Cities of Minneapolis and St. Paul with their major league sports, world-class museums and vibrant live entertainment options, Marc enjoys outdoor activities including hiking and snowshoeing on the north shore of Lake Superior, even during the long Minnesota winter.

Marc spent over 30 years in the travel industry specializing in sales and marketing for airlines and tour operators, and his desire to explore new places remains strong to this day. While he anticipated an eventual return to NYC, after discovering all that Minnesota had to offer, the decision to permanently make the Twin Cities his home was not a difficult one.

# HOW TO USE THIS BOOK

The Greater Than a Tourist book series was written by someone who has lived in an area for over three months. The goal of this book is to help travelers either dream or experience different locations by providing opinions from a local. The author has made suggestions based on their own experiences. Please do your own research before traveling to the area in case the suggested places are unavailable.

# FROM THE PUBLISHER

Traveling can be one of the most important parts of a person's life. The anticipation and memories that you have are some of the best. As a publisher of the Greater Than a Tourist book series, as well as the popular 50 Things to Know book series, we strive to help you learn about new places, spark your imagination, and inspire you. Wherever you are and whatever you do I wish you safe, fun, and inspiring travel.

Lisa Rusczyk Ed. D.
CZYK Publishing

# OUR STORY

Traveling is a passion of the "Greater than a Tourist" series creator. Lisa studied abroad in college, and for their honeymoon Lisa and her husband toured Europe. During her travels to Malta, an older man tried to give her some advice based on his own experience living on the island since he was a young boy. She was not sure if she should talk to the stranger but was interested in his advice. When traveling to some places she was wary to talk to locals because she was afraid that they weren't being genuine. Through her travels, Lisa learned how much locals had to share with tourists. Lisa created the "Greater Than a Tourist" book series to help connect people with locals. A topic that locals are very passionate about sharing.

# WELCOME TO
# > TOURIST

*"Do not follow where the path
may lead. Go instead where there is
no path and leave a trail"*

-Ralph Waldo Emerson

# 1. WHY MINNESOTA?

Perish the thought that there is snow on the ground
year-round and that it's always cold. Nothing could
be further from the truth. Yes, winter temperatures
can be brutal, especially in the northern third of the
state, but June through August is typically warm, and
sometimes even hot. On average, the Twin Cities
experiences 13 days each summer of 90 degrees or
higher. Over the last three decades there have been as
few as nine and as many as 34, 90+ days.

# 2. WHERE TO BEGIN YOUR PLANNED VISIT

With 5.6 million people statewide including 3.5
million in the Twin Cities metro area, there clearly
are many reasons so many people call Minnesota

home. For visiting purposes, think of the Minneapolis/St. Paul metro area as one primary area, and what is commonly called "outstate" as the other. If you're coming here for a professional sporting event, concert, or other cultural experience, chances are you'll be in the MSP (airport code) area. If fishing, hunting, winter sports, boating, golf, or just quiet time at one of the more than 10,000 lakes in the state is the plan, outstate is where you'll most likely be.

The Minneapolis/St. Paul International Airport is the likely Minnesota arrival point for a majority of visitors. As the second largest hub for Delta Air Lines (Atlanta is first), MSP offers nearly 600 daily flights on Delta alone, with other major carriers serving the area including Southwest, American, United, Alaska, Jet Blue and Spirit. Internationally, Delta serves most major Canadian cities direct from MSP, as well Tokyo, London, Amsterdam, Paris, Rome, and Reykjavik (Iceland). Delta will be adding Seoul non-stops, and Aer Lingus plans Dublin non-stops beginning in the summer of 2019. KLM flies to MSP from Amsterdam as well, as does Air France from Paris. Condor offers seasonal Frankfurt service.

Locally based Sun Country Airlines, though a small carrier, offers additional opportunities to fly to the Twin Cities from cities around the U.S.

# 3. HOW TO SURVIVE A WINTER VISIT

Sure, there is ample snow and cold during most winters which sometimes seem to go on for too long, but Minnesotans handle it with vim and vigor. Once you've lived here a few years, you acclimate just as in any other climate. So, if you're visiting in the winter, just dress in layers and you'll stay warm and toasty. While warm clothing including gloves and hat that covers the ears are no-brainers, be sure to have shoes/boots that won't slide on the ice or snow. Covered parking is plentiful in both downtowns, and underground heated parking is available in many office buildings.

# 4. THE BEST TIME TO VISIT

For guaranteed warm weather, it's summer, which also features generally comfortable evenings. Summer is most popular for golf, biking, hiking, Twins baseball, strolling the lakes or portaging lake-to-lake at the Boundary Waters Canoe Area. If cold weather is your thing for winter sports including skiing, ice fishing, snowmobiling and so on, December through March are the prime months. Spring and fall can be unpredictable weather-wise, especially early spring which can still be winter-like, and late fall, which can also resemble winter. But late spring and early autumn can be spectacular, not only with the changing foliage, but with comfortable days in the 60's and 70's and overnight low's in the 50's. All you'll for these times is a light coat or sweatshirt. It isn't unusual to have a few days in the 80's into late September.

# 5. BEST AREAS TO STAY – MSP

While there are hotels virtually everywhere in the metro area, four areas will serve visitors best. Each offers hotels in all price categories:

- Minneapolis downtown – Twins baseball, Vikings football, Timberwolves basketball, Orchestra Hall, live theaters: Guthrie, Orpheum, State, Pantages, Cowles. The entertainment and business heart of the Twin Cities. Best also for Minneapolis Institute of Art, First Avenue, U of M sporting events. Expect to pay for parking.

- St. Paul downtown – State Capitol, Ordway and Fitzgerald (MPR) theaters, Xcel Energy Center for Wild hockey and concerts, Saints minor league baseball at CHS Field, Science Museum, Children's Museum, Minnesota History Center, St. Paul Chamber Orchestra. Expect to pay for parking.

- Bloomington "strip" – just west of the airport, includes five mile stretch along I-494 from 34th Ave. to MN-100/Normandale Road. Mall of America (MOA) with more than 400 stores is at 24th Ave. Dozens of hotels and dining spots line this highway. Free parking. MOA alone has 13,000 spaces and also offers valet parking.

- St. Louis Park – suburb just five minutes west of downtown Minneapolis via I-394. Area offers about 15 hotels and many popular dining spots in the West End complex at Xenia Ave./Park Place exit.

Free parking, including underground heated garage at the West End.

# 6. GETTING AROUND TOWN BY METRO TRANSIT

The Twin Cities has two convenient and efficient light rail lines.

The Blue Line runs from the Mall of America in Bloomington to both passenger terminals at MSP Airport, and continues onward to U.S. Bank Stadium (Vikings football and concerts), downtown Minneapolis, with its terminus at Target Field (Twins baseball).

The Green Line runs from downtown St. Paul to downtown Minneapolis; a distance of 10 miles. Trains stop at the State Capitol, the new 20,000 seat Allianz Stadium (major league soccer) in St. Paul's Midway area, the University of Minnesota, as well as U.S. Bank Stadium, downtown Minneapolis and Target Field.

Metro Transit operates hundreds of bus routes throughout the Twin Cities area which may be more convenient for getting closer to your ultimate destination, especially if it is outside of the core downtowns.

# 7. GETTING AROUND TOWN BY UBER, LYFT OR TAXI

As in any other major metropolitan area, private car services are plentiful around-the-clock. Literally thousands of Uber, Lyft and taxi vehicles are at your beckon call via their respective apps. And for those who want a more private experience, there are several luxury limousine services who will drive you around town incognito.

# 8. GETTING AROUND TOWN BY AUTOMOBILE

Locals joke that Minnesota has just two seasons. Winter and road construction. As in any large metropolitan area, there are oodles of options when it comes to major highways and byways but do check ahead as there is bound to be a major construction site somewhere along the way. And yes, construction is on-going even during the winter. For example, the exit from northbound I-35 to westbound I-94 in downtown Minneapolis is currently closed for two years, as the intersection is being totally re-built. There are always alternative routes, but you should expect heavy traffic from 7-9 a.m. and 3-6 p.m. Monday through Friday on most major arteries. And on some, like I-494 through Bloomington, there can be high volume traffic all day long. Planning ahead and utilizing your GPS will help to keep you calm.

Outstate driving, as you would expect, is a more relaxing experience. However, if you're headed outstate from the Twin Cities, during afternoon rush hour (3-6 p.m.) in most any direction, in particular on Thursdays and Fridays via I-94 or I-35 northbound during the summer months, you should anticipate slow-and-go traffic well beyond the 494/694 loop around the MSP core. These routes are the most popular for "up north" cabin and resort travelers, especially in the direction of Brainerd, Duluth and the north shore of Lake Superior.

Once you get a fair distance out of the metro area, traffic will ease up and you'll be on your way. Better yet, leave earlier in the day and avoid most of the heavier traffic hours.

Travelers returning to the Twin Cities metro area from the north on Sunday afternoon and early evening can expect heavy traffic, too. Again, if you want to avoid creeping along with thousands of other cars, leave earlier on Sunday or consider returning to MSP on Monday.

# 9. BEST PLACES TO GRAB SOME GROCERIES

The largest grocery chain in the Twin Cities is Cub Foods, which also has locations outstate in St. Cloud, Rochester, Duluth and Mankato. Coborn's is a large chain that is primarily outstate, with the Twin Cities also the home to several upscale Lunds & Byerly's and Kowalski's, HyVee, Whole Foods, Trader Joe's and Fresh Thyme stores. There is no shortage of grocery stores, with many stores even having locations in the heart of downtown. Nearly 40,000 people live in downtown Minneapolis, so having Whole Foods, Trader Joe's, as well as Lund's and Byerly's there is super convenient. St. Paul also has a downtown population, albeit smaller, but Lund's and Byerly's is also there.

# 10. BEST LIQUOR STORES

The largest selection and generally lowest prices will be found at Total Wine, a national chain that arrived in Minnesota a couple of years ago. Their eight stores are all in suburban locales surrounding the inner core of the metro area. Haskell's is a local company also with stores throughout the metro, including downtown Minneapolis. Surdyk's has just a single store in Northeast Minneapolis, across the river from downtown, but it has an amazing selection of beer, wine and spirits. Attached is a superb cheese shop. There's an abundance of independent liquor stores around town, plus those at Costco (no membership required for a liquor purchase), Target, Trader Joe's, Whole Foods and Fresh Thyme. Several suburban municipalities have city-owned liquor stores, but their pricing is generally higher and their selection not as extensive. Towns in this category include Edina, Lakeville, Apple Valley and Mound in the metro area, and about 50 additional outstate locations.

# 11. MINNESOTA'S LOVE AFFAIR WITH BREW PUBS

Minnesotans love their beer, with craft breweries continuing to open across the state in large cities and small towns. Wherever you are, there's bound to be one within a reasonable distance. Best known in Minneapolis are Surly, Fulton, Lakes & Legends, and Boom Island; in St. Paul you can't go wrong at Lake Monster, Summit, Vine Park or the Urban Growler. Suburban favorites include Steel Toe in St. Louis Park, LTD in Hopkins, Bald Man in Eagan, Barley John's in New Brighton, and Lift Bridge in Stillwater.

Popular outstate micro-breweries include Copper Trail in Alexandria (also known as "Alex"), Bent Paddle and Lake Superior in Duluth, Jack Pine in Baxter, Gull Dam in Nisswa, August Schell in New Ulm, Forager in Rochester, Beaver Island in St. Cloud, Three Twenty in Pine City, and Voyageur in Grand Marais. Many of these local breweries now offer a nice lineup of food, while others sponsor various food trucks on select days of the week. Check ahead to see what is offered on the particular day if food is important to you.

# 12. MUSEUMS FOR THE YOUNG, NOT SO YOUNG, AND IN-BETWEEN

As the cultural center of the Upper Midwest, Minnesota, and especially the Twin Cities has no shortage of great museums to explore. Here are the most popular in the metro area;

• St. Paul – Minnesota, Children's Museum, Minnesota Science Museum, Minnesota History Center. These are located downtown. On the St. Paul campus of the University of Minnesota is the spectacular new Bell Museum and Planetarium.

• Minneapolis – still on the east side of the Mississippi River, but on the University of Minnesota Minneapolis campus, is the Frederick R. Weisner Art Museum, designed by Frank Gehry.

• On the west side of the Mississippi are the world-renowned Minneapolis Institute of Art (MIA), the Walker Art Center, adjacent Minneapolis Sculpture Garden and the Mill City Museum which is just down the street from the Guthrie Theater. The Minnesota Children's Theatre is part of the MIA complex in Minneapolis, just a few minutes south of downtown.

# 13. SPECIALTY MUSEUMS

If you're looking for something out of the ordinary, check out Prince's home and recording studio in suburban Chanhassen which has been turned into a Graceland-type museum. Guided tours take you through Prince's private production facilities and estate. Everything purple imaginable is on display, as well as other artifacts from his all too short life. Prince died in 2016 at the age of 57. Other unique venues outside of the metro area are the International Wolf Center "up north" in Ely; Hormel's SPAM Museum (yes, SPAM), in Austin; the Great Lakes Aquarium on Duluth's lakefront; the National Eagle Center on the Mississippi River flyway in the southeastern city of Wabasha; the Mille Lacs Indian Museum & Trading Post in Onamia; and the U.S. Hockey Hall of Fame in Eveleth.

# 14. GREAT PLACES TO TAKE A WALK

Some of my favorite places in St. Paul to take a stroll, jog or bike include Summit Avenue, offering long stretches of stately 19th and 20th century mansions, winding Mississippi River Blvd. with views across from St. Paul to Minneapolis, or at Como Park, Zoo & Conservatory in St. Paul. Crossing over the Mississippi there's Lake Nokomis, Lake Harriet, Lake of the Isles and Bde Maka Ska (formerly Lake Calhoun), all in south Minneapolis. Minnehaha Parkway is a beautiful stretch too, as it too winds for several miles across south Minneapolis, with the central creek ending as the spectacular Minnehaha Falls, emptying into the Mississippi River. Other popular options include the Minneapolis Sculpture Garden at the Walker Art Center, or you can walk endlessly in the downtown skyway systems of St. Paul or Minneapolis, staying out of the elements, shopping and dining along the way.

# 15. MINNESOTA LANDSCAPE ARBORETUM

The incredible 1,225-acre arboretum is well worth a visit to suburban Chanhassen. The "Arb" is just minutes away from Prince's Paisley Park, making for a memorable full-day. One of the premier arboretums in the U.S., this University of Minnesota-operated site is full of beautiful gardens and hiking trails, prairies, woods and northern tier tree collections. It is also viewable via an internal roadway that slowly winds its way throughout. The arboretum is approximately a 20-minute drive from Bloomington, or half an hour from downtown Minneapolis. Figure on about 40 minutes from downtown St. Paul.

# 16. BIKE TRAILS GALORE

There are hundreds of miles of well-maintained trails throughout the state, so if you're driving to Minnesota, bring your bike. In the MSP metro area, trails are everywhere. The Greenway runs across the full width of south Minneapolis, and there are trails virtually anywhere that there's a river or lake. Mississippi River Blvd. and Como Park in St. Paul are beautiful rides, and in Minneapolis, the trails around Lake Harriet, Mde Bada Ska (formerly Lake Calhoun) and Lake of the Isles are connected so that you can bike for miles and miles. Being a very bike friendly area, you'll also find many major roadways with specifically designated bicycle lanes, including right through the heart of the two downtowns. Bicycle racks are offered at all major locations including Target Field, Target Center and U.S. Bank Stadium, so bring a lock along for security.

There are several excellent internet sites that detail the seemingly endless biking opportunities around the state. Check out Explore Minnesota, Rails-to-Trails and Trail Link. The State of Minnesota site via the Department of Natural Resources, www.dnr.state.mn.us, gives information about biking in the Minnesota State Parks.

Minnesota's outstate bicycle trails are named so that you can search for them individually online or view them on a map. The most popular state trails according to various sites as well as fellow bikers are: 1/Root River (60 miles); 2/Paul Bunyan (120 miles); 3/Heartland (49 miles); 4/Willard Munger (160 miles); 5/Lake Wobegon (62 miles); 6/Central Lakes (55 miles); 7/Mesabi (115 miles); 8/Luce Line (63 miles); 9/Gitchi-Gami (88 miles); 10/Cannon Valley (20 miles).

Clearly, Minnesotan's are serious about their biking, and the vast statewide network is another reason why so many visiting bicyclists come here annually. Many of the trails are converted to snowmobile and cross-country skiing trails during the winter. And, yes, there are even quite a few hearty souls who bike all through the winter to work, no matter what the temperature may be.

# 17. THE STATE FAIR – EVERYTHING IMAGINABLE ON A STICK

For 12 days each year ending on Labor Day, "The Great Minnesota Get-Together", aka the Minnesota State Fair, welcomes more than two million visitors to the largest state fair, based on daily attendance, in the U.S. There's something for everyone at this one-of-a-kind venue, from farm exhibits, to rides and games on the Midway, top name concerts, and the most amazing collection of food-on-a-stick that you'll ever see. Don't miss the incredible chocolate chip cookies at Sweet Martha's Chocolate Cookie Jar!

Also, at the fair are hundreds of booths sponsored by organizations from around the state. Farming, plus livestock and horse exhibitors are a huge part of the fair, with an animal birthing center complete with video streaming one of the most visited venues. Rural 4-H clubs are well represented, too, bringing their cattle, sheep and goats, rabbits, swine, poultry and other animals to the fair for presentation.

The creative arts are also well represented with limitless shopping opportunities. Free live stage shows are scattered around the fair, often with big name entertainers performing. But no doubt, the #1 thing to do at the Minnesota State Fair is people-watch. So, grab some grub, perhaps a local craft brew, find a seat along the Midway, and take in the crowd. It's like nothing you've ever seen before. Short, tall, thin, not so thin, diverse races and ethnicities are all represented, and everyone gets along.

The huge crowds, often more than 200,000 people on a single day, makes for limited parking at the fair itself. While you can find a place to park, it may be expensive. Metro Transit offers express bus service from dozens of locations around the Twin Cities, and for a very reasonable round-trip fare. Buses start early in the day and run a busy schedule until late at night.

# 18. SWEET DESSERT SPOTS

If you're looking for something sweet with your morning coffee or after dinner, there are a slew of great options. St. Paul's Grand Old Creamery, Café Latte, and Bread & Chocolate are within a few blocks of one another on Grand Avenue. There's Sebastian Joe's Ice Cream in Minneapolis, or if you're more of a pastry person, you can't beat Patisserie 46, which has won international baking competitions, even in Paris! Other great spots include any of four locations of Snuffy's Malt Shop, or Patrick's Bakery Cafe in Richfield and Maple Grove. If you're driving to Duluth from MSP, Toby's cinnamon rolls are a must at the Hinckley exit along I-35. Heading on I-94 toward Alexandria you'll want to check out Charlie's Café in Freeport, popular for caramel rolls and pies.

And, if you can't find exactly what you're looking for, chances are there's one of Minnesota's own, Dairy Queen, someplace nearby.

# 19. WE HOPE YOU LIKE COFFEE

The number one gathering spot across the state is the local coffee shop. Hardly a deal is struck without first discussing it over coffee. Locally based Caribou Coffee seems to be everywhere, but you'll also find scores of Starbucks locations, and just as many independent shops, primarily in St. Paul and Minneapolis proper. Every town in Minnesota, big and small, has at least one, and often several coffee shops to sip, chat and relax. Business meetings that take place in a coffee shop often go for an hour or longer, and there is still no resolution to a problem or proposed working arrangement. This is where "let me think about it" or "I'll get back to you" come into the equation. Passive aggressive to be sure, you betcha, but it's all part of the oft-stated "Minnesota Nice" syndrome, where we're too nice and don't want to hurt anyone's feelings, in person.

# 20. HOW TO ACT PASSIVE AGGRESSIVE

Trying to get a firm commitment from a Minnesotan can be a very frustrating thing. Rather than tell you to your face that he or she isn't really interested or disagrees with what you are proposing, whether it be business related or something personal, be prepared to hear, Spoken slowly, "That's….different" (instead of saying your idea is stupid), "interesting", "I'm not sure", "let me think about it" or "I'll get back to you". Then, rather than hurting your feelings face-to-face, a real Minnesotan will often tell you "no thanks", via email, text or voicemail. It's all part of being non-confrontational and kind. And it will drive you crazy if you don't have experience with this type of non-committal behavior.

# 21. BEST PLACES FOR LIVE MUSIC

Live music can be found all over the Twin Cities, and in lots of outstate locales, too, including many casinos. Some of the most popular clubs include First Avenue, made famous by Prince, the adjacent 7th Avenue Entry, Dakota Jazz Club, Lee's Liquor Lounge, the Cabooze and the Fine Line, all in Minneapolis. St. Paul offers up the Palace Theater, Wild Tymes and the Turf Club. For a full listing of weekly happenings, pick up a copy of City Pages, or visit their website. During the summer the Minnesota Zoo outdoor amphitheater offers evening concerts by well-known national musicians, and there are free concerts under the stars at the Lake Harriet Bandshell in Minneapolis.

# 22. ART SHOWS, ART GALLERIES AND MORE

The arts are alive and well around the state. Outstate, check out the shops and galleries in Grand Marais, Nisswa, Duluth, Detroit Lakes and Red Wing. St. Paul's "Lowertown" and Northeast Minneapolis are jammed with lofts and artist studios. And each summer, the Uptown and Edina art fairs feature hundreds of booths with talented artisans selling their truly exceptional creations. The Northeast Art Crawl, "Art-A-Whirl" is something you won't want to miss if you're in MSP in mid-May. Other annual art fairs include the eclectic Loring Park Art Fair, Powderhorn (a neighborhood in Minneapolis) and the St. Anthony art fairs. Smaller art fairs are held in towns and cities around the state, mostly during the summer months.

If you're looking for some wacky wares, as well as nicely made small artisan items, consider a visit to the Minnesota Renaissance Festival, held annually from mid-August through September, weekends only, in Jordan, a short drive southwest of the Twin Cities.

With more than 250 vendors and 320,000 annual visitors, you're bound to have a great time.

# 23. VISITING THE BRAINERD LAKES AND NISSWA AREA

This beautiful area, chock full of lakes and small towns is one of the most popular for Twin Cities residents who head north throughout the summer. Just two hours away if you can avoid the guaranteed Friday afternoon and Sunday evening traffic jams, aside from literally thousands of personal cabins on scores of area lakes, there are fabulous resorts that feature everything you'd want in a getaway. Golf (often multiple courses), an in-house spa, multiple restaurants, boating, fishing, lakes and indoor pools, bonfires, watersports, and much more are typically available, along with rustic to deluxe accommodations. While there are dozens upon dozens of small, rustic "resorts" within a 3-4 hour drive from the Twin Cities, each with a half dozen to 10 or 12 cabins, larger properties with extensive facilities include Grand View Lodge at Gull Lake, Breezy Point, Madden's, Cragun's, Kavanaugh's, Quarterdeck, and Arrowwood Resort in Alexandria.

# 24. MINNESOTA'S STATE PARKS

People come to Minnesota from all over the country to enjoy our 75 state parks. With so much wilderness around the state, there's something for everyone. Hiking, camping, biking, swimming, waterfalls, spectacular vistas, birdwatching, canoeing, rock climbing, and so much more are all available. There's also an excellent chance that you'll come across deer, elk, maybe even a moose or wolves along the way. During the peak summer months and fall foliage weekends, you'll want to reserve a campsite if you plan to stay in one of the parks. The more popular parks can fill up several months in advance. The comprehensive state website, www.dnr.state.mn.us/state_parks is your best source of information.

# 25. TRY YOUR LUCK

Minnesota has 21 Native American-run casinos in 17 counties around the state, some with hundreds of hotel rooms attached. Some of the most popular are Mystic Lake in suburban Prior Lake, Grand Casino with locations in Hinckley and on the shore of Lake Mille Lacs, Jackpot Junction in Morton, Black Bear in Carlton (en route to Duluth from MSP), and Treasure Island just outside of Red Wing. In addition to casino gambling, enjoy concerts, often by famous entertainers, and a selection of dining venues. The casinos are a great getaway from the Twin Cities for just about anyone, and are kid-friendly with activity centers and indoor pools.

# 26. BOUNDARY WATERS CANOE AREA WILDERNESS

There are so many superlatives to describe the BWCA, that you need to experience it for yourself. This densely forested and remote area in Minnesota's Arrowhead, the northeast area of the state above Lake Superior, is a world unto its own. Located within the Superior National Forest, the BWCA consists of more than one million acres of wilderness that is so large that it includes the 65-mile long Border Trail. If you're looking for an easily accessible escape from humanity, this is the place. And, surprisingly, the park welcomes just a little over 100,000 annual visitors, so it is never crowded. You will be immersed by thick, lush forests, endless lakes and streams, all kinds of wildlife, and total silence. Except, perhaps, for the sound of the wind and howling wolves. The BWCA is an absolute treasure that shouldn't be missed. If you're not a camper, you can still explore the area by staying in a resort or hotel on the Lake Superior shoreline in Lutsen or Grand Marais.

# 27. LAKE SUPERIOR'S SPECTACULAR NORTH SHORE

Probably my favorite part of the state, the 145 miles of U.S. Highway 61 made famous by Minnesota's own Bob Dylan (Robert Zimmerman), from Duluth to the Canadian border is a spectacularly beautiful and rugged. The largest towns along the way are Two Harbors with just 3,600 residents, and scenic Grand Marais with its population of a mere 1,339. Both offer great shops and local dining options. Between the two is the incredible rocky shoreline of Lake Superior, the largest of the Great Lakes, as well as scores of cabins, resorts and small hotels. There are also larger hotel and condo options like Superior Shores, Lutsen Resort with indoor pools, fireplaces, and more extensive dining options adjacent to the Lutsen ski area. Our family favorite for many years has been the rustic and friendly Solbakken Resort, due to its affordability and proximity, directly on Lake Superior. Gooseberry Falls, Split Rock Lighthouse and numerous hiking and biking trails along the way make for a memorable and guaranteed quiet getaway.

# 28. DULUTH

This lakefront city at the far western end of Lake Superior is a favorite of Minnesotans for a long-weekend getaway. Duluth offers plenty to do year-round, though Lake Superior is never warm enough for swimming. Just up highway 61 to the northeast are the village of Two Harbors, a fun stopping point for shopping or a quick meal, as well as Split Rock Lighthouse, Gooseberry Falls and the Temperance River. Duluth is the ideal home base with numerous hotels located on the waterfront by the scenic lift bridge, but the city itself offers great hilltop views and some excellent dining options. Colder than the Twin Cities most of the year due to its location on the Lake, indoor pools are an expectation at area hotels. If downhill skiing is your thing, Spirit Mountain is the place. Located on the hill just to the west of Duluth with 22 runs over 175 acres, other winter sports include snowboarding, fat biking and snowtubing. Spirit Mountain is a year-round adventure area with non-winter activities including an adventure park and mountain biking trails. Just 150 miles north of the Twin Cities on I-35, its superb location is just 10 minutes from downtown Duluth and the lakefront hotels, restaurants and entertainment venues.

# 29. TWIN CITIES FOOD FROM RESTAURANTS TO FOOD TRUCKS

The Twin Cities restaurant scene has improved immeasurably over the last decade. As the MSP area has become more diverse, with immigrants arriving by the tens of thousands from southeast Asia, Africa, Europe and south of the border, dining options have changed, too. Nicollet Avenue in south Minneapolis from Franklin Avenue to 28th Street has been dubbed "Eat Street", and is jammed with Greek, Mexican, Vietnamese, Himalayan and an eclectic mix of pizza joints, diners (our favorite is "Bad Waitress"), and African cuisine, too. Both cities have great restaurants from casual to fine dining. The infamous Minnesota supper club, "J.D. Hoyt's" in the North Loop of Minneapolis is always superb, and St. Paul's "W.A. Frost" and "Joan's in the Park" are two excellent choices for a memorable experience.

Grand Avenue in St. Paul is a fun and extensive area for restaurants and shopping. From Dale Street on the east to Fairview Avenue on the west, you will find all kinds of food options, casual and bit more upscale, though nothing extravagant. Minnesota's staple, lake walleye, is served up in numerous ways by the Tavern on Grand, with other restaurants ranging from the local diner, Uptowner Grill, to Café Latte, a very popular cafeteria-style hotspot with everything homemade from soups to incredible desserts. It also features a wine bar with creative pizzas. Other places you may want to check out include The Lexington, Brasa, La Cucaracha, Bread & Chocolate, the original Green Mill, Everest on Grand (Nepalese) and the always organic New French Café, which unlike the original spot in Minneapolis, offers full table service at the location just down the street from Macalester College.

Being a somewhat larger and more energetic city, Minneapolis has a more diverse culinary scene, with popular options downtown, in the North Loop/Warehouse District, Northeast, Uptown and in south Minneapolis. While it is extremely difficult to nearly impossible to recommend where you should go, I will at least name a few of our favorites. Pizza

Nea in Northeast, just a couple of blocks across the Mississippi from downtown, is our go-to place for consistently good and creative pizza. Black Sheep Pizza is also a top-rated spot, with multiple locations. Owned and operated by local chef Hector Ruiz, Rincon 38, Café Ena and La Fresca, all on Grand Avenue south of Lake Street (he also has Costa Blanca in Northeast), are variations on Caribbean, Mexican, or Spanish cuisine, and all are fabulous. A few other names to consider: Victor's 1959 Cuban Cafe, Lake & Irving, Stella for seafood and a fantastic rooftop bar in Uptown, Wakame Sushi & Asian Bistro, Monte Carlo, the Lowry, Café Lurcat, and the list could go on and on. These are just a few of our favorites.

In recent years the food truck craze has taken the Twin Cities by storm. You name the type of food, and there's probably a truck serving it here. Both downtowns see line-ups of trucks in the morning as they stake their position for the midday lunch crowd. You'll also find food trucks from a huge number of brick and mortar restaurants, spreading their name and a few foods, too, in areas beyond their physical location. Others, still, sit at brew pubs, sporting events, along busy highways, at fairs, festivals and

even weddings. Some of the more creative names
we've come across in the Twin Cities include:

- The Anchor Fish 'n Chips
- Potter's Pasties
- A Cupcake Social
- Motley Crews Heavy Metal Grill
- Chicks on Wheels
- Meat & Greet MN
- Asian Invasion

# 30. BUNDLE UP!

If you're contemplating a winter visit to Minnesota, and there are lots of reasons that you should, be sure to pack warm gloves, a warm hat that covers your ears, a scarf, boots with good traction, and you'll also do well with a hooded sweatshirt and a warm sweater or two. Plan on dressing in layers during the coldest weather and you'll be amazed just how toasty you can be. You probably won't need all of the above items but arrive prepared and you'll have a great time. It is truly invigorating to take a walk on a crisp and sunny winter day.

The popular book, "Bring Warm Clothes", published in 1991, kind of sums it all up, especially if you are coming here during the colder months. But cold weather doesn't keep a Minnesotan indoors. Snow doesn't either. A few inches of the white stuff may mean leaving for your destination a bit earlier than usual or waiting for the traffic to let up. Statewide, snow removal expertise is revered. We can have six inches overnight, and by the time we get going in the morning, the roads have been plowed. Of course, there's always that pile at the end of the driveway that needs to be dug through before departing. Sometimes several times as the plows come back over and over again, as needed.

# 31. A MAJOR LEAGUE SPORTS MECCA

Only a handful of U.S. metro areas have all four major sports leagues – Twins baseball (MLB), Vikings football (NFL), Wild hockey (NHL), Timberwolves basketball (NBA), and the Twin Cities is one of them. Major League Soccer's (MLS) Minnesota United is also here, getting ready to play at the newly built Allianz Field in St. Paul. If you're still looking for more, there's the WNBA's Lynx, and University of Minnesota Big Ten sports including football at TCF Stadium, basketball at William's Arena (The Barn), and ice hockey, women's (Ridder Arena), and men's (Mariucci Arena). Last, but not least, thoroughbred horse racing takes places late spring through summer at Canterbury Park in suburban Shakopee.

# 32. BEAUTIFUL LAKE MINNETONKA

The largest metro area lake by far, the nearly 15,000-acre Lake Minnetonka is a favorite water playground throughout the summer months. The quaint towns of Excelsior and Wayzata both lie along its shores, offering high quality shops and restaurants nearby. Made up of dozens of bays and inlets, Lake Minnetonka, especially on weekends but also to a slightly lesser extent during the week in the evening, is packed with hundreds of personal pleasure craft as well as larger tour boats with dining on board. The lake starts just 15 miles west of downtown Minneapolis, an easy drive from the western half of the MSP area. Several restaurants, including Maynard's in Excelsior, have parking for cars in the front and boats on the back dock.

# 33. SKYWAYS, SKYWAYS, SKYWAYS

Walking the skyways is the easiest, warmest and driest way to get around downtown St. Paul and Minneapolis, and even Rochester and Duluth have skyway systems to help you stay warm (or cool) and out of the elements. Walk for countless blocks from one end of Minneapolis or St. Paul to the other without having to go outside. Leave your coat in the car or your hotel room if staying downtown, finding everything you need at skyway level, one floor above the frigid or sweltering sidewalks.

# 34. GO APE AT MINNESOTA'S ZOOS

The Minnesota Zoo is in Apple Valley, a south suburb about 15 minutes from the airport and Bloomington strip. In St. Paul, Como Park Zoo & Conservatory are located adjacent to one another. Other popular animal venues include the Lake Superior Zoo and Great Lakes Aquarium in Duluth, as well as Sea Life Aquarium at the Mall of America.

# 35. POPULAR LOCAL APPS

Download the apps that interest you to get the low-down on what's going on in Minnesota: StarTribune, Minnesota Twins, Minnesota Wild, Minnesota Timberwolves, City Pages, Explore Minnesota Photo, Twin Cities Live, Duluth News-Tribune, Minnesota State Fair, Minnesota Beer Finder, WCCO, KARE, KMSP, KSTP, Minnesota Public Radio, Superior National Forest, Metro Transit, Minnesota State Parks, Nice Ride Minnesota, Lime – Your Ride Anytime. Available only in print format, Lavender is the free weekly of the LBGTQ community, and available throughout the MSP area.

# 36. THE BEST OF LOCAL MEDIA

The two major newspapers in the Twin Cities are the StarTribune and St. Paul Pioneer Press. Both have excellent websites that detail just about anything you want to know about the area. The Duluth News-Tribune is the largest paper in the northern part of the state, and also has a wide-ranging website. City Pages is the largest entertainment weekly with complete listings of just about anything going on around the area. You can pick up a free copy in hundreds of locations or check them out online. Available only in print format, Lavender is the free weekly of the LBGTQ community, and available throughout the MSP area.

# 37. BABE, BEMIDJI AND BEYOND

If you'd like a picture with Paul Bunyan and Babe the blue ox, head to the south shore of Lake Bemidji in north central Minnesota. Home to Bemidji State University, Bemidji is the largest town in the region with about 15,000 residents. Lake Bemidji is the northernmost lake feeding the Mississippi River, with the headwaters of the river being about 30 miles to the southwest at Lake Itasca State Park. The nation's icebox, International Falls, is 113 miles to the northeast, on the Canadian border, via highway 71.

# 38. FORE!

With 575 golf courses, or one for about each 9,000 residents, Minnesota is in the top ten of golf states in the U.S. Even though we can only play outdoors from April through October annually, hitting the little white ball is insanely popular here. Courses are located throughout the MSP area, and there are scores of golf resorts convenient to lake country. The Ryder Cup was played in suburban Chaska in 2017 and will be returning in a few years. And, the PGA recently added an annual Minnesota stop to their tour.

For indoor practice, the Braemar Golf Dome in Edina is a two-level driving range that is warm and crowded all through the winter months. The first high-tech Topgolf entertainment center recently opened in north suburban Brooklyn Park, featuring a three-level driving range.

# 39. THE STATE OF HOCKEY

With the return of NHL hockey to Minnesota 1997 after what seemed like forever (the North Stars defected to Dallas in 1993), the new team coined the marketing line "The State of Hockey". You'll see and hear it everywhere, and Minnesotans do consider the game to be theirs from birth. You'll find indoor and outdoor night-lit rinks statewide, and where there's a high school, there's a team and local association sponsoring participation in the sport from the time a kid can walk.

# 40. WINTER SPORTS

Winter doesn't make Minnesotans stay indoors. In fact, quite the contrary. It just makes us move faster. Popular winter sports include hockey, skiing (downhill and cross-country), snowshoeing, ice fishing, curling, broomball, snowboarding, ice skating and snowmobiling. Snowtubing is also offered at Minnesota's ski hills, as well as at some local parks. Check out Buck Hill, Hyland Hills and Afton Alps in the Twin Cities metro; Spirit Mountain and Lutsen Mountains in outstate.

# 41. OUTDOOR SUMMER ACTIVITIES

Minnesotans are extremely active year-round, but clearly summer is the time we get to spread our wings. Biking is part of the local culture, as the Twin Cities is considered the #1 bicycle friendly metro area in the country. And with so many lakes and rivers, too, we spend a lot of time fishing, boating, swimming and just getting wet any way that we can. Hiking, gardening, and attending outdoor concerts are also very popular during the summer months.

# 42. SPECTACULAR FALL FOLIAGE

Minnesota turns all shades of orange, yellow and red each autumn. Popular outstate areas to take in the change of seasons range from the North Shore along U.S. highway 61, the St. Croix River Valley from Taylors Falls to Stillwater, and along the Mississippi River from the Twin Cities south to Red Wing, Winona and La Crosse.

# 43. NO, DOROTHY, THIS ISN'T FARGO

Just so you can tell your friends back home the truth, yes, Judy Garland of "The Wizard of Oz" fame, was born and raised in Grand Rapids, Minnesota. No, Mary Tyler Moore was not from Minnesota, but her much-loved "Mary Tyler Moore Show" was set in Minneapolis. A statue of her tossing her hat in the air just as she did in the show's opening, is located on Nicollet Mall in downtown. Lastly, the Coen Brothers movie "Fargo", was filmed in various Minnesota locations, but the accents are from somewhere else. Who knows where? The Coen Brothers grew up in the Minneapolis suburb of St. Louis Park, which was also the boyhood home of former senator and SNL writer/actor, Al Franken, and journalist/author Thomas Friedman (no relation).

# 44. BIKE AND SCOOTER RENTAL

Nice Ride and Lime Bike bicycle rentals, Bird and Lime scooter rentals are available throughout both downtowns, as well as in some busier neighborhoods. This is a very affordable and fun way to get around, and you can pickup and drop-off virtually anywhere. However, to be truly safe, bring along a helmet as these are not provided or available with rental.

# 45. FAMOUS MINNESOTANS

Just in case you were wondering: Prince, Hubert Humphrey, Judy Garland, Kevin McHale, Bob Dylan, F. Scott Fitzgerald, Jesse "The Body" Ventura, Garrison Keillor, Josh Harnett, Jessica Lange, Charles Schulz, Herb Brooks, Sinclair Lewis, Warren Burger, John Madden, Al Franken, Joel and Ethan Coen, Winona Ryder, Roger Maris, William and Charles Mayo, Walter Mondale.

# 46. ANNUAL HAPPENINGS

Some of the most highly attended festivals and such include: Minnesota Renaissance Festival, Grand Old Day (St. Paul), Irish Festival (St. Paul), Uptown Art Fair, Edina Art Fair, Loring Park Art Fair, Powderhorn Art Festival, St. Paul Winter Carnival, Twin Cities Marathon (1st weekend in October) is dubbed "The Most Beautiful Urban Marathon in America", Basilica Block Party (July 4th weekend), Northern Spark, Bayfront Blues Festival (Duluth), Minnesota State Fair, Minneapolis Aquatennial, Stone Arch Bridge Festival (Minneapolis), Duluth Dylan Fest.

Also, from Memorial Day through Labor Day, ValleyFair Amusement Park offers 75 rides and attractions including a water park and eight roller coasters. The suburban Shakopee venue remains open weekends-only through September.

# 47. LIVE ON STAGE

Large venue facilities in Minneapolis include US Bank Stadium (the Vikings Stadium holds 70,000), Target Field (40,000), Target Center (20,000), Orchestra Hall, the Orpheum, State, Pantages and Cowles Center theaters. The Xcel Energy Center (20,000) in St. Paul is also a popular concert destination. The Fitzgerald (MPR) and Ordway theaters are also in downtown St. Paul.

# 48. KAYAK AND CANOE RENTAL

Having 10,000+ lakes around the state means endless opportunities to enjoy water sports. Kayak, canoe, paddle-boat, sea-doo, motorboat and pontoon boat rentals are available at scores of locations including Como Lake in St. Paul and Bde Maka Ska (formerly Lake Calhoun)/Lake of the Isles in Minneapolis, as well as around the state.

# 49. GREAT BREAKFAST SPOTS

Some of our favorite breakfast places are Eggy's, The Lowry, Victor's 1959 Café (Cuban) and The Egg and I (Lyndale Ave. location) in Minneapolis. We also frequent Fat Nat's in New Hope. Bad Waitress, Hazel's Northeast, the Hen House and any location of Key's also specialize in breakfast fare. On the St. Paul side of town there's the New French Café just one block from Macalester College, the Highland Grill, The Buttered Tin in Lowertown, and the Uptowner Café on Grand.

# 50. THE GUTHRIE THEATER

The world-famous Guthrie is a stunning, start-of-the-art facility built just a few years ago. The neighborhood around it has evolved into a trendy and popular community on the northern edge of downtown Minneapolis, with great restaurants and modern high-rise apartments in abundance nearby. Named for Sir Tyrone Guthrie, since 1963 the Guthrie has been not only a leading producer of original plays, but also an origination point for shows with their sights set on Broadway. Be sure to experience not only their incredible performances, but

61

also the upper level cantilevered outdoor balcony which overlooks the Mississippi River below. The backstage tour (reservations required) is a fascinating hour-long look behind the scenes at theater production.

# BONUS 51. HOW TO SPEAK MINNESOTAN

Here are some uniquely Minnesota sayings that you may come across during your visit:

"Do you want to come with?" (come with what?), "you betcha", "let's meet for coffee", "I'll get back to you" (meaning I'm really not interested but don't want to tell you to your face), "up north", "going to the lake", "hot dish" (i.e. casserole), "We're going to the Cities" (meaning the metro area), "borrow me", "pop" instead of soda, "meat raffle" which is just what it sounds like, often at the local VFW, "dontcha know", "interesting" (not really, but I don't know what else to say without offending you), "oh for cute", "borrow me" (this one is very painful to hear), and perhaps my biggest pet peeve with Minnesota-talk is that natives cannot differentiate between saying "me" or "I" during a sentence that shows possessiveness. "Me and my friend were…..",,, "you and me should….", "let's you and I go….", and so on. Ouch!

# TOP REASONS TO BOOK THIS TRIP

Lakes, lakes, and more lakes. Water, water, everywhere

Boundary Waters Canoe Area/Minnesota's North Shore – spectacular scenic beauty like no where else in the U.S.

The Twin Cities: World-class museums, dining and entertainment, major league sports, a friendly/diverse/progressive community

# BONUS BOOK

# 50 THINGS TO KNOW ABOUT PACKING LIGHT FOR TRAVEL

## PACK THE RIGHT WAY EVERY TIME

## AUTHOR: MANIDIPA BHATTACHARYYA

Edited by Melanie Howthorne

# ABOUT THE AUTHOR

Manidipa Bhattacharyya is a creative writer and editor, with an education in English literature and Linguistics. After working in the IT industry for seven long years she decided to call it quits and follow her heart instead. Manidipa has been ghost writing, editing, proof reading and doing secondary research services for many story tellers and article writers for about three years. She stays in Kolkata, India with her husband and a busy two year old. In her own time Manidipa enjoys travelling, photography and writing flash fiction.

Manidipa believes in travelling light and never carries anything that she couldn't haul herself on a trip. However, travelling with her child changed the scenario. She seemed to carry the entire world with her for the baby on the first two trips. But good sense prevailed and she is again working her way to becoming a light traveler, this time with a kid.

# INTRODUCTION

*He who would travel happily
must travel light.*

-Antoine de Saint-Exupéry

Travel takes you to different places from seas and mountains to deserts and much more. In your travels you get to interact with different people and their cultures. You will, however, enjoy the sights and interact positively with these new people even more, if you are travelling light.

When you travel light your mind can be free from worry about your belongings. You do not have to spend precious vacation time waiting for your luggage to arrive after a long flight. There is be no chance of your bags going missing and the best part is that you need not pay a fee for checked baggage.

People who have mastered this art of packing light will root for you to take only one carry-on, wherever you go. However, many people can find it really hard to pack light. More so if you are travelling with children. Differentiating between "must have" and "just in case" items is the starting point. There will be ample shopping avenues at your destination which are just waiting to be explored.

This book will show you 'packing' in a new 'light' –
pun intended –  and help you to embrace light
packing practices for all of your future travels.

Off to packing!

# DEDICATION

I dedicate this book to all the travel buffs that I know,
who have given me great insights into the contents of
their backpacks.

# THE RIGHT TRAVEL GEAR

## 1. CHOOSE YOUR TRAVEL GEAR CAREFULLY

While selecting your travel gear, pick items that are
light weight, durable and most importantly, easy to
carry. There are cases with wheels so you can drag
them along – these are usually on the heavy side
because of the trolley. Alternatively a backpack that
you can carry comfortably on your back, or even a
duffel bag that you can carry easily by hand or sling
across your body are also great options. Whatever
you choose, one thing to keep in mind is that the
luggage itself should not weigh a ton, this will give
you the flexibility to bring along one extra pair of
shoes if you so desire.

# 2. CARRY THE MINIMUM NUMBER OF BAGS

Selecting light weight luggage is not everything. You need to restrict the number of bags you carry as well. One carry-on size bag is ideal for light travel. Most carriers allow one cabin baggage plus one purse, handbag or camera bag as long as it slides under the seat in front. So technically, you can carry two items of luggage without checking them in.

# 3. PACK ONE EXTRA BAG

Always pack one extra empty bag along with your essential items. This could be a very light weight duffel bag or even a sturdy tote bag which takes up minimal space. In the event that you end up buying a lot of souvenirs, you already have a handy bag to stuff all that into and do not have to spend time hunting for an appropriate bag.

> *I'm very strict with my packing and have everything in its right place. I never change a rule. I hardly use anything in the hotel room. I wheel my own wardrobe in and that's it.*
>
> Charlie Watts

# CLOTHES & ACCESSORIES

## 4. PLAN AHEAD

Figure out in advance what you plan to do on your trip. That will help you to pick that one dress you need for the occasion. If you are going to attend a wedding then you have to carry formal wear. If not, you can ditch the gown for something lighter that will be comfortable during long walks or on the beach.

## 5. WEAR THAT JACKET

Remember that wearing items will not add extra luggage for your air travel. So wear that bulky jacket that you plan to carry for your trip. This saves space and can also help keep you warm during the chilly flight.

## 6. MIX AND MATCH

Carry clothes that can be interchangeably used to reinvent your look. Find one top that goes well with a couple of pairs of pants or skirts. Use tops, shirts and jackets wisely along with other accessories like a scarf or a stole to create a new look.

# 7. CHOOSE YOUR FABRIC WISELY

Stuffing clothes in cramped bags definitely takes its toll which results in wrinkles. It is best to carry wrinkle free, synthetic clothes or merino tops. This will eliminate the need for that small iron you usually bring along.

# 8. DITCH CLOTHES PACK UNDERWEAR

Pack more underwear and socks. These are the things that will give you a fresh feel even if you do not get a chance to wear fresh clothes. Moreover these are easy to wash and can be dried inside the hotel room itself.

# 9. CHOOSE DARK OVER LIGHT

While picking your clothes choose dark coloured ones. They are easy to colour coordinate and can last longer before needing a wash. Accidental food spills and dirt from the road are less visible on darker clothes.

# 10. WEAR YOUR JEANS

Take only one pair of Jeans with you, which you should wear on the flight. Remember to pick a pair that can be worn for sightseeing trips and is equally eloquent for dinner. You can add variety by adding light weight cargoes and chinos.

## 11. CARRY SMART ACCESSORIES

The right accessory can give you a fresh look even with the same old dress. An intelligent neck-piece, a couple of bright scarves, stoles or a sarong can be used in a number of ways to add variety to your clothing. These light weight beauties can double up as a nursing cover, a light blanket, beach wear, a modesty cover for visiting places of worship, and also makes for an enthralling game of peek-a-boo.

## 12. LEARN TO FOLD YOUR GARMENTS

Seasoned travellers all swear by rolling their clothes for compact and wrinkle free packing. Bundle packing, where you roll the clothes around a central object as if tying it up, is also a popular method of compact and wrinkle free packing. Stacking folded clothes one on top of another is a big no-no as it makes creases extreme and they are difficult to get rid of without ironing.

# 13. WASH YOUR DIRTY LAUNDRY

One of the ways to avoid carrying loads of clothes is to wash the clothes you carry. At some places you might get to use the laundry services or a Laundromat but if you are in a pinch, best solution is to wash them yourself. If that is the plan then carrying quick drying clothes is highly recommended, which most often also happen to be the wrinkle free variety.

# 14. LEAVE THOSE TOWELS BEHIND

Regular towels take up a lot of space, are heavy and take ages to dry out. If you are staying at hotels they will provide you with towels anyway. If you are travelling to a remote place, where the availability of towels look doubtful, carry a light weight travel towel of viscose material to do the job.

# 15. USE A COMPRESSION BAG

Compression bags are getting lots of recommendation now days from regular travellers. These are useful for saving space in your luggage when you have to pack bulky dresses. While packing for the return trip, get help from the hotel staff to arrange a vacuum cleaner.

# FOOTWEAR

## 16. PUT ON YOUR HIKING BOOTS

If you have plans to go hiking or trekking during your trip, you will need those bulky hiking boots. The best way to carry them is to wear them on flight to save space and luggage weight. You can remove the boots once inside and be comfortable in your socks.

## 17. PICKING THE RIGHT SHOES

Shoes are often the bulkiest items, along with being the dainty if you are a female. They need care and take up a lot of space in your luggage. It is advisable therefore to pick shoes very carefully. If you plan to do a lot of walking and site seeing, then wearing a pair of comfortable walking shoes are a must. For more formal occasions you can carry durable, light weight flats which will not take up much space.

## 18. STUFF SHOES

If you happen to pack a pair of shoes, ensure you utilize their hollow insides. Tuck small items like rolled up socks or belts to save space. They will also be easy to find.

# TOILETRIES

## 19. STASHING TOILETRIES

Carry only absolute necessities. Airline rules dictate
that for one carry-on bag, liquids and gels must be in
3.4 ounce (100ml) bottles or less, and must be packed
in a one quart zip-lock bag. If you are planning to stay
in a hotel, the basic things will be provided for you.
It's best is to buy the rest from the local market at
your destination.

## 20. TAKE ALONG TAMPONS

Tampons are a hard to find item in a lot of countries.
Figure out how many you need and pack accordingly.
For longer stays you can buy them online and have
them delivered to where you are staying.

## 21. GET PAMPERED BEFORE YOU TRAVEL

Some avid travellers suggest getting a pedicure and
manicure just the day before travelling. This not only
gives you a well kept look, you also save the trouble
of packing nail polish.  Remember, every little bit of
weight reduced adds up.

# ELECTRONICS

## 22. LUGGING ALONG ELECTRONICS

Electronics have a large role to play in our lives today. Most of us cannot imagine our lives away from our phones, laptops or tablets. However while travelling, one must consider the amount of weight these electronics add to our luggage. Thankfully smart phones come along with all the essentials tools like a camera, email access, picture editing tools and more. They are smart to the point of eliminating the need to carry multiple gadgets. Choose a smart phone that suits all your requirements and travel with the world in your palms or pocket.

## 23. REDUCE THE NUMBER OF CHARGERS

If you do travel with multiple electronic devices, you will have to bear the additional burden of carrying all their chargers too. Check if a single charger can be used for multiple devices. You might also consider investing in a pocket charger. These small devices support multiple devices while keeping you charged on the go.

# 24. TRAVEL FRIENDLY APPS

Along with smart phones come numerous apps, which are immensely helpful in our travels. You name it and you have an app for it at hand – take pictures, sharing with friends and family, torch to light dark roads, maps, checking flight/train times, find hotels and many other things. Use these smart alternatives to traditional items like books to eliminate weight and save space.

*I get ideas about what's essential*
*when packing my suitcase.*

-Diane von Furstenberg

## TRAVELLING WITH KIDS

## 25. BRING ALONG THE STROLLER

Kids might enjoy walking for a while but they soon tire out and a stroller is the just the right thing for them to rest in while you continue your tour. Strollers also double duty as a luggage carrier and shopping bag holder. Remember to pick a light weight, easy to handle brand of stroller. Better yet, find out in advance if you can rent a stroller at your destination.

# 26. BRING ONLY ENOUGH DIAPERS FOR YOUR TRIP

Diapers take up a lot of space and add to the weight of your luggage. Therefore it is advisable to carry just enough diapers to last through the trip and a few for afterwards, till you buy fresh stock at your destination. Unless of course you are travelling to a really remote area, in which case you have no choice but to carry the load. Otherwise diapers are something you will find pretty easily.

# 27. TAKE ONLY A COUPLE OF TOYS

Children are easily attracted by new things in their environment. While travelling they will find numerous 'new' objects to scrutinize and play with. Packing just one favorite toy is enough, or if there is no favorite toy leave out all of them in favor of stories or imaginary games.

# 28. CARRY KID FRIENDLY SNACKS

Create a small snack counter in your bag to store away quick bites for those sudden hunger pangs. Depending on the child's age this could include chocolates, raisins, dry fruits, granola bars or biscuits. Also keep a bottle of water handy for your little one.

These things do not add much weight and can be adjusted in a handbag or knapsack.

## 29. GAMES TO CARRY

Create some travel specific, imaginary games if you have slightly grown up children, like spot the attractions. Keep a coloring book and colors handy for in-flight or hotel time. Apps on your smart phone can keep the children engaged with cartoons and story books. Older children are often entertained by games available on phones or tablets. This cuts the weight of luggage down while keeping the kids entertained.

## 30. LET THE KIDS CARRY THEIR LOAD

A good thing is to start early sharing of responsibilities. Let your child pick a bag of his or her choice and pack it themselves. Keep tabs on what they are stuffing in their bags by asking if they will be using that item on the trip. It could start out being just an entertainment bag initially but with growing years they will learn to sort the useful from the superfluous. Children as little as four can maneuver a small trolley suitcase like a pro- their experience in pull along toys credit. If you are worried that you may be pulling it for them, you may want to start with a backpack.

# 31. DECIDE ON LOCATION FOR CHILDREN TO SLEEP

While on a trip you might not always get a crib at your destination, and carrying one will make life all the more difficult. Instead call ahead to see if there are any cribs or roll out beds for children. You may even put blankets on the floor. Weave them a story about camping and they will gladly sleep without any trouble.

# 32. GET BABY PRODUCTS DELIVERED AT YOUR DESTINATION

If you are absolutely paranoid about not getting your favourite variety of diaper or brand of baby food, check out online stores like amazon.com for services in your destination city. You can buy things online ahead of your travel and get them delivered to your hotel upon arrival.

# 33. FEEDING NEEDS OF YOUR INFANTS

If you are travelling with a breastfed infant, you save the trouble of carrying bottles and bottle sanitization kits. For special food, or medications, you may need to call ahead to make sure you have a refrigerator where you are staying.

# 34. FEEDING NEEDS OF YOUR TODDLER

With the progression from infancy to toddler, their dietary requirements too evolve. You will have to pack some snacks for travelling time. Fresh fruits and vegetables can be purchased at your destination. Most of the cities you travel to in whichever part of the world, will have baby food products and formulas, available at the local drug-store or the supermarket.

# 35. PICKING CLOTHES FOR YOUR BABY

Contrary to popular belief, babies can do without many changes of clothes. At the most pack 2 outfits per day. Pack mix and match type clothes for your little one as well. Pick things which are comfortable to wear and quick to dry.

# 36. SELECTING SHOES FOR YOUR BABY

Like outfits, kids can make do with two pairs of comfortable shoes. If you can get some water resistant shoes it will be best. To expedite drying wet shoes, you can stuff newspaper in them then wrap

them with newspaper and leave them to dry
overnight.

# 37. KEEP ONE CHANGE OF CLOTHES HANDY

Travelling with kids can be tricky. Keep a change of
clothes for the kids and mum handy in your purse or
tote bag. This takes a bit of space in your hand
luggage but comes extremely handy in case there are
any accidents or spills.

# 38. LEAVE BEHIND BABY ACCESSORIES

Baby accessories like their bed, bath tub, car seat, crib
etc. should be left at home. Many hotels provide a
crib on request, while car seats can be borrowed from
friends or rented. Babies can be given a bath in the
hotel sink or even in the adult bath tub with a little bit
of water. If you bring a few bath toys, they can be
used in the bath, pool, and out of water. They can also
be sanitized easily in the sink.

# 39. CARRY A SMALL LOAD OF PLASTIC BAGS

With children around there are chances of a number
of soiled clothes and diapers. These plastic bags help
to sort the dirt from the clean inside your big bag.

These are very light weight and come in handy to other carry stuff as well at times.

# PACK WITH A PURPOSE

## 40. PACKING FOR BUSINESS TRIPS

One neutral-colored suit should suffice. It can be paired with different shirts, ties and accessories for different occasions. One pair of black suit pants could be worn with a matching jacket for the office or with a snazzy top for dinner.

## 41. PACKING FOR A CRUISE

Most cruises have formal dinners, and that formal dress usually takes up a lot of space. However you might find a tuxedo to rent. For women, a short black dress with multiple accessory options will do the trick.

## 42. PACKING FOR A LONG TRIP OVER DIFFERENT CLIMATES

The secret packing mantra for travel over multiple climates is layering. Layering traps air around your body creating insulation against the cold. The same light t-shirt that is comfortable in a warmer climate can be the innermost layer in a colder climate.

## REDUCE SOME MORE WEIGHT

## 43. LEAVE PRECIOUS THINGS AT HOME

Things that you would hate to lose or get damaged leave them at home. Precious jewelry, expensive gadgets or dresses, could be anything. You will not require these on your trip. Leave them at home and spare the load on your mind.

## 44. SEND SOUVENIRS BY MAIL

If you have spent all your money on purchasing souvenirs, carrying them back in the same bag that you brought along would be difficult. Either pack everything in another bag and check it in the airport or get everything shipped to your home. Use an international carrier for a secure transit, but this could be more expensive than the checking fees at the airport.

## 45. AVOID CARRYING BOOKS

Books equal to weight. There are many reading apps which you can download on your smart phone or tab.

Plus there are gadgets like Kindle and Nook that are thinner and lighter alternatives to your regular book.

# CHECK, GET, SET, CHECK AGAIN

## 46. STRATEGIZE BEFORE PACKING

Create a travel list and prepare all that you think you need to carry along. Keep everything on your bed or floor before packing and then think through once again – do I really need that? Any item that meets this question can be avoided. Remove whatever you don't really need and pack the rest.

## 47. TEST YOUR LUGGAGE

Once you have fully packed for the trip take a test trip with your luggage. Take your bags and go to town for window shopping for an hour. If you enjoy your hour long trip it is good to go, if not, go home and reduce the load some more. Repeat this test till you hit the right weight.

## 48. ADD A ROLL OF DUCT TAPE

You might wonder why, when this book has been talking about reducing stuff, we're suddenly asking you to pack something totally unusual. This is because when you have limited supplies, duct tape is immensely helpful for small repairs – a broken bag, leaking zip-lock bag, broken sunglasses, you name it and duct tape can fix it, temporarily.

# 49. LIST OF ESSENTIAL ITEMS

Even though the emphasis is on packing light, there are things which have to be carried for any trip. Here is our list of essentials:

•Passport/Visa or any other ID

•Any other paper work that might be required on a trip like permits, hotel reservation confirmations etc.

•Medicines – all your prescription medicines and emergency kit, especially if you are travelling with children

•Medical or vaccination records

•Money in foreign currency if travelling to a different country

•Tickets- Email or Message them to your phone

# 50. MAKE THE MOST OF YOUR TRIP

Wherever you are going, whatever you hope to do we encourage you to embrace it whole-heartedly. Take in the scenery, the culture and above all, enjoy your time away from home.

*On a long journey even a straw weighs heavy.*

-Spanish Proverb

# PACKING AND PLANNING TIPS

### A Week before Leaving

- Arrange for someone to take care of pets and water plants.

- Stop mail and newspaper.

- Notify Credit Card companies where you are going.

- Change your thermostat settings.

- Car inspected, oil is changed, and tires have the correct pressure.

- Passports and photo identification is up to date.

- Pay bills.

- Copy important items and download travel Apps.

- Start collecting small bills for tips.

### Right Before Leaving

- Clean out refrigerator.

- Empty garbage cans.

- Lock windows.

- Make sure you have the proper identification with you.

- Bring cash for tips.

- Remember travel documents.

- Lock door behind you.

- Remember wallet.

- Unplug items in house and pack chargers.

# READ OTHER
# GREATER THAN A TOURIST
# BOOKS

Greater Than a Tourist San Miguel de Allende Guanajuato Mexico:
50 Travel Tips from a Local by Tom Peterson

Greater Than a Tourist – Lake George Area New York USA:
50 Travel Tips from a Local by Janine Hirschklau

Greater Than a Tourist – Monterey California United States:
50 Travel Tips from a Local by Katie Begley

Greater Than a Tourist – Chanai Crete Greece:
50 Travel Tips from a Local by Dimitra Papagrigoraki

Greater Than a Tourist – The Garden Route Western Cape Province
South Africa: 50 Travel Tips from a Local by Li-Anne McGregor van
Aardt

Greater Than a Tourist – Sevilla Andalusia Spain:
50 Travel Tips from a Local by Gabi Gazon

Greater Than a Tourist – Kota Bharu Kelantan Malaysia:
50 Travel Tips from a Local by Aditi Shukla

Children's Book: Charlie the Cavalier Travels the World by Lisa
Rusczyk

# > TOURIST

Visit Greater Than a Tourist for Free Travel Tips
  http://GreaterThanATourist.com

Sign up for the Greater Than a Tourist Newsletter for
  discount days, new books, and travel information:
  http://eepurl.com/cxspyf

Follow us on Facebook for tips, images, and ideas:
  https://www.facebook.com/GreaterThanATourist

Follow us on Pinterest for travel tips and ideas:
  http://pinterest.com/GreaterThanATourist

Follow us on Instagram for beautiful travel images:
  http://Instagram.com/GreaterThanATourist

# > TOURIST

Please leave your honest review of this book on Amazon and Goodreads. Please send your feedback to GreaterThanaTourist@gmail.com as we continue to improve the series. We appreciate your positive and constructive feedback. Thank you.

# METRIC CONVERSIONS

## TEMPERATURE

| | |
|---|---|
| 110° F — | — 40° C |
| 100° F — | |
| 90° F — | — 30° C |
| 80° F — | |
| 70° F — | — 20° C |
| 60° F — | |
| 50° F — | — 10° C |
| 40° F — | |
| 32° F — | — 0° C |
| 20° F — | |
| 10° F — | — -10° C |
| 0° F — | — -18° C |
| -10° F — | |
| -20° F — | — -30° C |

### To convert F to C:

Subtract 32, and then multiply by 5/9 or .5555.

### To Convert C to F:

Multiply by 1.8 and then add 32.

### 32F = 0C

## LIQUID VOLUME

To Convert:...................Multiply by
U.S. Gallons to Liters................ 3.8
U.S. Liters to Gallons .................26
Imperial Gallons to U.S. Gallons 1.2
Imperial Gallons to Liters....... 4.55
Liters to Imperial Gallons ........22
**1 Liter = .26 U.S. Gallon**
**1 U.S. Gallon = 3.8 Liters**

## DISTANCE

To convert ............Multiply by
Inches to Centimeters ....2.54
Centimeters to Inches ........39
Feet to Meters....................... .3
Meters to Feet ...................3.28
Yards to Meters ..................91
Meters to Yards ................1.09
Miles to Kilometers ..........1.61
Kilometers to Miles............ .62
**1 Mile = 1.6 km**
**1 km = .62 Miles**

## WEIGHT

1 Ounce = .28 Grams
1 Pound = .4555 Kilograms
1 Gram = .04 Ounce
1 Kilogram = 2.2 Pounds

# TRAVEL QUESTIONS

- Do you bring presents home to family or friends after a vacation?

- Do you get motion sick?

- Do you have a favorite billboard?

- Do you know what to do if there is a flat tire?

- Do you like a sun roof open?

- Do you like to eat in the car?

- Do you like to wear sun glasses in the car?

- Do you like toppings on your ice cream?

- Do you use public bathrooms?

- Did you bring your cell phone and does it have power?

- Do you have a form of identification with you?

- Have you ever been pulled over by a cop?

- Have you ever given money to a stranger on a road trip?

- Have you ever taken a road trip with animals?

- Have you ever went on a vacation alone?

- Have you ever run out of gas?

- If you could move to any place in the world, where would it be?

- If you could travel anywhere in the world, where would you travel?

- If you could travel in any vehicle, which one would it be?

- If you had three things to wish for from a magic genie, what would they be?

- If you have a driver's license, how many times did it take you to pass the test?

- What are you the most afraid of on vacation?

- What do you want to get away from the most when you are on vacation?

- What foods smells bad to you?

- What item do you bring on ever trip with you away from home?

- What makes you sleepy?

- What song would you love to hear on the radio when you're cruising on the highway?

- What travel job would you want the least?

- What will you miss most while you are away from home?

- What is something you always wanted to try?

- What is the best road side attraction that you ever saw?

- What is the farthest distance you ever biked?

- What is the farthest distance you ever walked?

- What is the weirdest thing you needed to buy while on vacation?

- What is your favorite candy?

- What is your favorite color car?

- What is your favorite family vacation?

- What is your favorite food?

- What is your favorite gas station drink or food?

- What is your favorite license plate design?

- What is your favorite restaurant?

- What is your favorite smell?

- What is your favorite song?

- What is your favorite sound that nature makes?

- What is your favorite thing to bring home from a vacation?

- What is your favorite vacation with friends?

- What is your favorite way to relax?

- Where is the farthest place you ever traveled in a car?

- Where is the farthest place you ever went North, South, East and West?

- Where is your favorite place in the world?

- Who is your favorite singer?

- Who taught you how to drive?

- Who will you miss the most while you are away?

- Who if the first person you will contact when you get to your destination?

- Who brought you on your first vacation?

- Who likes to travel the most in your life?

- Would you rather be hot or cold?

- Would you rather drive above, below, or at the speed limited?

- Would you rather drive on a highway or a back road?

- Would you rather go on a train or a boat?

- Would you rather go to the beach or the woods?

# TRAVEL BUCKET LIST

1.

2.

3.

4.

5.

6.

7.

8.

9.

10.

# NOTES

Made in United States
Troutdale, OR
02/11/2024

17594318R00072